cooking the ISRAELI way

The tangy juice of fresh lemons makes North African chicken soup a special addition to this Sabbath meal. (Recipe on pages 40 and 41.)

cooking the
ISRAELI way

JOSEPHINE BACON

PHOTOGRAPHS BY ROBERT L. & DIANE WOLFE

easy menu
ethnic
cookbooks

Lerner Publications Company ▪ Minneapolis

Drawings and Map by Jeanette Swofford

Additional photographs are reproduced through the courtesy of Israel Ministry of Tourism, p. 10; Audrey Giesen, p. 13.

The page border for this book is based on the pomegranate, an ancient fruit known to the Hebrews in Biblical times. Pomegranates are still grown in Israel today.

To Hanna, my favorite daughter

Library of Congress Cataloging-in-Publication Data

Bacon, Josephine.
  Cooking the Israeli way.

  (Easy menu ethnic cookbooks)
  Includes index.
  Summary: An introduction to the cooking of Israel including such traditional recipes as cheese blintzes, turkey schnitzel, felafel in pita, and poppyseed cake. Also includes information on the geography, customs, and people of the middle eastern country.
  1. Cookery, Israeli—Juvenile literature. 2. Cookery, Jewish—Juvenile literature. 3. Israel—Juvenile literature. [1. Cookery, Israeli. 2. Israel—Social life and customs] I. Wolfe, Robert L., ill. II. Wolfe, Diane., ill. III. Title. IV. Series.
TX724.B225 1986   641.595694   85-18059
ISBN 0-8225-0912-1 (lib. bdg.)

Manufactured in the United States of America

    3 4 5 6 7 8 9 10 94 93 92 91

Russian salad is a tasty combination of a wide variety of ingredients from apples to mushrooms. (Recipe on page 32.)

CONTENTS

Vegetables

Rift Valley

Fish

Haifa

Sea of Galilee

Avocados

Nazareth

Coastal
Plains

Melons

Tomatoes

Turkeys

Figs
Dates

Tel Aviv-
Yafo

Jordan River

Chickens

Jerusalem

Cows

Citrus Fruits

Judeo-Galilean
Highlands

Dead Sea

Sheep

Dairy
Products

Rift Valley

Mediterranean Sea

Negev Desert

Sheep

Lambs

Flag of Israel

INTRODUCTION

Israel is a country with a very unusual heritage. It is the ancient land of the Bible, the setting for the events described in the scriptures sacred to both Jews and Christians. Because of this Biblical connection, the names of Israel's cities—Jerusalem, Haifa, Bethlehem, Nazareth—are as familiar to most Americans as are the names of cities in the United States. At the same time, Israel is a very new nation, established in 1948. It is the modern homeland of the Jewish people, the only country in the world where Judaism is the major religion and where most of the population is Jewish.

The food of Israel is as unique as the history of the country. It is a blend of many different cooking traditions, combining Middle Eastern and European influences with a uniquely Jewish flavor.

THE LAND

Israel is a very small country, only one-fourth the size of the state of Maine. It occupies a narrow strip of land 265 miles (424 kilometers) long at the eastern end of the Mediterranean Sea. The climate of the country resembles that of southern California. Except at higher elevations, where it is often cold enough to snow, it has hot, dry summers and short, mild winters.

The northernmost part of Israel, Upper Galilee, is quite mountainous. Lower Galilee is a fertile plain watered by the Sea of Galilee, which is actually a large freshwater lake with a few saltwater wells in it. The River Jordan connects the Sea of Galilee with a true saltwater lake, the Dead Sea, which is the saltiest body of water in the world and also the lowest point on the face of the earth—1,310 feet (399 meters) below sea level.

The central part of Israel is the most fertile, especially the area of the Coastal Plains called the Plain of Sharon. It is here that the famous Jaffa oranges are grown. To the east of the Coastal Plains lies the Judeo-Galilean Highlands, with historic Jerusalem standing atop one of the high, rolling hills. To the south is the Negev Desert, whose dry soil is quite fertile when irrigated. Further south, the land drops sharply away to the Arava, a desert much like California's Death Valley, where the climate is so dry and the earth so salty that very little will grow there.

THE PEOPLE

Like the United States, Israel has a population made up largely of immigrants or descendants of immigrants. Only a small minority of present-day Israelis lived in the country before independence in 1948; even fewer have lived in the area for more than 100 years.

It was in the late 1800s that Jews first began returning to the region then called Palestine, the site of their historic homeland in the Middle East. These early immigrants, known as Zionists, were determined to establish a Jewish state in the area, a state where all Jews would be guaranteed entry and safety from persecution. Most of the earliest settlers came from Russia and Poland, but Zionist movements soon sprang up all over Europe and in the United States, and small numbers of Jews from these areas also found their way to Palestine. After Palestine was partitioned and the state of Israel established in 1948, the Jewish population of the new nation doubled in size.

The 3.7 million Jews who live in Israel today have come from almost every country in the world. Among them are refugees who fled Europe during World War II to escape the Nazi plan to exterminate Jews. Others came from Arab countries of the Middle East where hostility toward Jews increased greatly after the establishment of the state of Israel. Today a large part of Israel's Jewish population traces its origins to Arab and other Muslim countries in the Middle East and North Africa.

Although about 83 percent of the people of Israel are Jewish, there is a large Muslim Arab population in cities such as Nazareth and Galilee, as well as other minorities including Druse and Armenians. Jerusalem, which is a holy city for Muslims, Christians, and Jews, is home to members of all three religious groups.

While it has not been easy for Israel to make one nation out of people from so many different regions and cultures, language has been one unifying factor. The official language of Israel is Hebrew, an ancient tongue that is the language of the Old Testament. Hebrew has changed to some extent over the centuries, but today an Israeli can read the original

Hebrew words of the Bible almost as easily as an American can read the daily newspaper.

The army is another unifying element in Israeli life. Because Israel is surrounded by unfriendly neighbors, military service is required of most of her citizens. Almost all young Israelis—men and women—spend two years in the army when they reach the age of 18. Israel's army is a great melting pot, bringing together people of different backgrounds who would never have met in civilian life.

THE FOOD

Israel's cuisine is as diverse as her people and reflects a combination of influences from all over the world. Because most of the country's population is Jewish, one of the strongest of these influences is the religious and cultural tradition shared by Jews everywhere.

The traditional dietary laws observed by Orthodox Jews have a strong influence on Israeli cooking. These dietary laws require that all food be kosher, which means "fit" or "proper." Orthodox Jews do not eat pork, shellfish, or some other animals, such as rabbits or hares. They also follow strict rules regarding the slaughtering of animals and the preparing of meat for human consumption. Another dietary law forbids the eating of dairy products at the same meal with meat. Orthodox Jewish households and all Israel's public institutions observe the dietary laws, serving kosher food and maintaining separate cooking utensils, tableware, and dishwashing facilities for milk and meat dishes.

Israeli cuisine has been shaped not only by Jewish tradition but also by the climate and the geography of the country. The kinds of foods grown in Israel and readily available are often featured in Israeli menus. For example, high-quality fruits and vegetables, which are abundant and very inexpensive, can be found at nearly every meal. Like many other countries of the Middle East, Israel also produces and consumes a wide variety of dairy products, including many forms of soured milk and yogurt.

In general, Israelis eat less meat than most Americans and Europeans do. While turkey and chicken are inexpensive in Israel, red meat is very costly and the quality is poor by

A vendor sells peaches at an open-air market.

U.S. standards. This is due partly to the demands of the dietary laws, which forbid the consumption of many parts of meat animals, and partly to the dry climate and lack of grazing land. Because of the scarcity of meat, many Israelis limit their diets to vegetables, fruits, and dairy products, although some are vegetarians because of health reasons and a concern for animal welfare.

THE ISRAELI FESTIVAL YEAR

Life in Israel is strongly influenced by the yearly cycle of Jewish religious festivals. Many of these holidays are observed by Jews all over the world, but they have a special meaning in Israel because they are based on the ancient agricultural calendar once common to all people of the Middle East. The religious festivals also influence Israeli cuisine since each is usually marked by the eating of certain kinds of foods. During the festivals, these foods are on sale by street vendors everywhere, so even visitors to Israel know that something special is happening.

The festival year begins in September or October with the Jewish New Year (Rosh Hashanah), the first of a group of observances called the High Holidays. On Rosh Hashanah, it is traditional to eat sweet foods such as apples and honeycake. Ten days later, on the Day of Atonement (Yom Kippur), no food is eaten for 24 hours. This solemn day is followed by an 8-day harvest festival called the Feast of Tabernacles (Sukkot), when little booths are built and decorated with fruits and flowers. Tabernacles celebrates the arrival of the Children of Israel in the Holy Land. During this festival, dishes featuring harvest fruits and vegetables are eaten.

In the winter, around Christmastime, there is a minor holiday called the Festival of Lights (Hanukah). The candles of a candelabra called a menorah are lit one by one on each of the eight days of this festival. Oil-fried foods such as potato pancakes and doughnuts are traditional Hanukah treats.

The children's favorite festival is Purim, the Feast of Esther, in early spring. Although Purim is a normal work day in Israel, after working hours, young and old alike parade the streets in costume and go to parties. During this happy festival, people eat sweet cookies filled with poppy seeds or prunes. These treats, called Haman's Ears or Haman's Pockets (depending on their size), are named after the villain in the Biblical story of Esther.

The main spring festival is Passover (Pesach), one of three festivals of pilgrimage, and the holiday that Jesus was celebrating at the Last Supper. Nothing leavened with yeast may be eaten during this week-long festival, and yeast bread is replaced by matzo—a flat, unleavened cracker-like bread. On the first evening of Passover, there is a ritual banquet called the Seder, which commemorates the Exodus of the Jews from Egypt in Biblical times.

The last festival of the Jewish calendar is the Feast of Weeks (Shavuot), another 8-day festival. It celebrates the giving of the Tablets of the Law to Moses on Mount Sinai and is also known as the festival of the first fruits (Hag Habikkurim), when the first summer fruits and vegetables come into season. On this holiday, it is customary to eat dairy products such as cheese pancakes, as well as a cone-shape cake that represents Mount Sinai.

THE SABBATH: A SPECIAL DAY EVERY WEEK

In addition to the yearly cycle of festivals, Israelis have a small holiday every week when they celebrate the Sabbath. Beginning at sundown on Friday, the Sabbath is a special day of solemn religious services and joyous family gatherings. The Sabbath meal is an occasion looked forward to all week. Each family has its special dishes, which are prepared and served with loving care. Good food is an essential part of the Sabbath celebration, as it is of most aspects of Israeli life.

Mount Tabor rises behind rows of almond trees in full bloom.

BEFORE YOU BEGIN

Cooking any dish, plain or fancy, is easier and more fun if you are familiar with its ingredients. Israeli cooking makes use of some ingredients that you may not know. You should also be familiar with the special terms that will be used in various recipes in this book. Therefore, *before* you start cooking any of the Israeli dishes in this book, study the following "dictionary" of special ingredients and terms very carefully. Then read through the recipe you want to try from beginning to end.

Now you are ready to shop for ingredients and to organize the cookware you will need. Once you have assembled everything, you can begin to cook. It is also very important to read *The Careful Cook* on page 47 before you start. Following these rules will make your cooking experience safe, fun, and easy.

COOKING UTENSILS

colander— A bowl-shaped dish with holes in it that is used for washing or draining food *melon baller*—A utensil with a small rounded end for scooping round pieces from melons and other foods

sieve—A bowl-shaped utensil made of wire mesh used to wash or drain small, fine foods such as tea or rice

slotted spoon—A spoon with small openings in the bowl used to pick solid food out of a liquid

spatula—A flat, thin utensil, usually metal, used to lift, toss, turn, or scoop up food

COOKING TERMS

baste—To pour, brush, or spoon liquid over food as it cooks in order to flavor and moisten it

boil—To heat a liquid over high heat until bubbles form and rise rapidly to the surface

brown—To cook food quickly in fat over high heat so that the surface turns an even brown

garnish—To decorate with a small piece of food such as parsley

grate—To cut into tiny pieces by rubbing the food against a grater

knead—To work dough by pressing it with the palms, pushing it outward, and then pressing it over on itself

preheat—To allow an oven to warm up to a certain temperature before putting food in it

sauté—To fry quickly over high heat in oil or fat, stirring or turning the food to prevent burning

scald—To heat a liquid (such as milk) to a temperature just below its boiling point

SPECIAL INGREDIENTS

allspice—The berry of a West Indian tree, used whole or ground, whose flavor resembles a combination of cinnamon, nutmeg, and cloves.

chickpeas—A pale, round legume, available dried or canned

coriander seed—The seeds of an herb used both whole and ground to flavor foods

cumin seed—The seeds of an herb used to give food a pungent, slightly hot taste

Dijon-style mustard—A commercially prepared condiment (ingredient used to enhance the flavor of food) made from mustard seed, white wine, vinegar, salt, and spices

felafel *mix*—A dry mix of chickpeas, flour, and oriental spices

field beans—A variety of bean native to the Middle East. Often called Egyptian field beans, they are available at Middle Eastern stores, specialty stores, or some supermarkets.

halva—A sweet candy of crushed nuts or sesame seeds in honey syrup

matzo—Crisp unleavened bread eaten mainly at Passover by Jews around the world

matzo meal—Finely ground matzos

mint—Fresh or dried leaves of various mint plants used in cooking

olive oil—An oil made by pressing olives. It is used in cooking and for dressing salads.

paprika—A red seasoning made from ground dried pods of the *capsicum* pepper plant. It has a sweeter flavor than cayenne.

parsnip—The long, white, sweet-tasting root vegetable of the parsnip plant

pine nuts—The edible seed of certain pine trees

pita bread—Flat, round loaves of bread common throughout the Middle East. When baked, a puffed pocket of air forms in the center of bread.

poppy seed filling—A thick, sweet mixture made from poppy seeds and corn syrup used in making cakes, pies, and breads

saffron—A deep orange, aromatic spice made from the flower of the saffron plant

sesame seeds—Seed from an herb grown in tropical countries. They are often toasted before eating.

tahina—A paste of ground sesame seeds

turmeric—A yellow, aromatic spice made from the root of the turmeric plant

yeast—An ingredient used in baking that causes dough to rise

AN ISRAELI MENU

Below are simplified menu plans for typical Israeli meals. The Hebrew names of the dishes are given, along with a pronunciation guide. *Recipe included in book

ENGLISH	HEBREW	PRONUNCIATION GUIDE
Breakfast	**Arukhat Boker**	ah-roo-HAHT BO-care
I	I	
Orange Juice	Mitz Tapoozim	MEETS tah-poo-ZEEM
Fresh Fruits	Peirot Tri'im	pay-ROTE tree-EEM
Pickled Tuna	Lakiyerda	lah-kee-ARE-dah
*Israeli Salad	Salat Yisraeli	sah-LAHT yis-ray-LEE
Olives	Zitim	zee-TEEM
Roll	Lakhmaniya	lah-mah-nee-AH
Tea with Lemon	Teh Belimon	TAY beh-lee-MONE
II	II	
Grapefruit	Eshkolit	esh-ko-LEET
*Egg and Tomato Scramble	Shakshooka	shahk-SHOO-kah
Bread and Margarine	Lehem ve'margarina	LEH-hem veh-mar-gah-REE-nah
Orange Marmalade	Ribat Tapoozim	ree-BAHT tah-poo-ZEEM
Coffee	Kafeh	kah-FAY
Snacks	**Mata'amim**	mah-tah-MEEM
*Felafel in Pita	Felafel Bipita	feh-LAH-fel beh-PEE-tah
*Israeli Doughnuts	Soofganiyot	soof-gahn-ee-YOTE
Lunch	**Arukhat Tzohorayim**	ah-roo-HAHT tso-ho-RAH-yeem
I	I	
*Kibbutz Carrot Salad	Salat Gezer	sah-LAHT GEH-zer

ENGLISH	HEBREW	PRONUNCIATION GUIDE
*Baked Fish	Dag Bitanoor	DAHG beh-tah-NOOR
*Israeli Salad	Salat Yisraeli	sah-LAHT yis-ray-LEE
II	II	
Vegetable Soup	Marak Yerakot	mah-RAHK yeh-rah-KOTE
*Ground Meat with Sesame Sauce	Siniyeh	SEE-nee-yah
*Fruit Soup	Marak Peirot	mah-RAHK pay-ROTE
*Russian Salad	Salat Russi	sah-LAHT roo-SEE
*Cheese Blintzes	Levavot Gvina	leh-vay-VOTE g'vee-NAH
Fresh Fruit	Peirot	pay-ROTE

Vegetarian Meal — *Arukhat Tsimhonit* — ah-roo-HAHT tsim-hone-EET

Friday Night Dinner — *Arukhat Erev Shabbat* — ah-roo-HAHT AY-rev shah-BAHT

*Bean Soup	Marak Shu'it	mah-RAHK shoo-EET
*Turkey Schnitzel	Schnitzel Hodoo	SHNEE-tsel HO-doo
Fruit Salad	Salat Peirot	sah-LAHT pay-ROTE
*Poppy Seed Cake	Ugat Pereg	oo-GAHT PAY-reg

Saturday Midday Meal — *Arukhat Tzohorayim Bishabbat* — ah-roo-HAHT tso-ho-RAH-yeem beh-shah-BAHT

*Sabbath Stew	Dfina	deh-FEE-nah
Fresh Fruit	Peirot	pay-ROTE
Turkish Coffee	Kafeh Turki	kay-FAY tur-KEE
Cookies	Ugiyot	oo-ghee-YOTE

Passover Meal — *Seder* — SAY-der

Matzos	Matzot	mah-TZOTE
*North African Chicken Soup	Marak Off Mizarahi	mah-RAHK OAF miz-rah-KHEE
*Chicken Stuffed with Oranges	Off Memooleh Betapoozim	OAF meh-moo-LAY beh-tah-poo-ZEEM
*Melon Dessert	Liftan Melon	lif-TAHN meh-LONE
*Passover Matzo Layer Cake	Ugat Matzot	oo-GHAT mah-TZOTE

Most Israeli breakfast dishes, such as egg and tomato scramble *(left)* **and Israeli salad** *(right)*, **can be served at any meal.**

BREAKFAST/
Arukhat Boker

Breakfasts in Israel are hearty, especially in the countryside where they are eaten at the crack of dawn before a hard day's work in the fields. On Saturday, the Sabbath, when no cooking is permitted in orthodox Jewish households, the meal is a hearty brunch of cold foods such as olives, yogurt, breads, jams, various cheeses, and smoked and pickled fish. It is accompanied by lots of hot tea or coffee.

Israeli Salad/
Salat Yisraeli

Salad is eaten at almost every Israeli meal. On the kibbutz *(collective community), oil, lemon juice, and a bowl of whole vegetables are left on each table, and diners make their own individual salads so that they are absolutely fresh.*

2 tomatoes, chopped
1 cucumber, peeled and chopped
1 green pepper, seeded and chopped
4 tablespoons chopped fresh parsley
2 tablespoons olive oil
juice of 1 lemon (about 3 tablespoons)
½ teaspoon salt
¼ teaspoon pepper

1. In a large bowl, combine chopped tomatoes, cucumber, green pepper, and parsley. Sprinkle with olive oil and toss.
2. Add lemon juice, salt, and pepper to salad and toss again. Serve immediately.

Serves 4

Egg and Tomato Scramble/ Shakshooka

This dish was brought to Israel by Tunisian Jews, who like it very spicy. The amount of chili powder can be increased or decreased, depending on how hot you like it. Like most Israeli breakfast dishes, shakshooka *can be served at any meal. The tomato mixture can be made in advance and reheated before adding the eggs.*

1 14½-ounce can whole
    peeled tomatoes
¼ cup butter or margarine
1 teaspoon chili powder
1 tablespoon all-purpose flour
3 eggs
½ teaspoon salt

1. Place tomatoes in a colander and drain well. Transfer tomatoes to a bowl and break into small pieces with a spoon.

2. Melt butter or margarine in a deep skillet or saucepan. Add tomatoes, chili powder, and flour and stir until smooth.
3. Reduce heat to low and simmer, uncovered, very gently for 1 hour.
4. In a small bowl, beat together eggs and salt. Just before serving, add eggs to tomato mixture and stir lightly, cooking until eggs are set. Serve hot with pita bread.

Serves 4 to 6

SNACKS/
Mata'amim

Israelis are very busy people. They start work early in the morning—all offices are open at 8:00 A.M.—and eat lunch rather late, around 1:00 P.M. Snacking gives Israelis the energy they need to keep up their busy pace.

Felafel in Pita/
Felafel Bipita

Sidewalk food- and drink-sellers are common throughout the Middle East, and many of the snacks they sell are meals in themselves. Felafel, *considered Israel's national dish, is one such nutritious, filling snack food.*

  1 10-ounce package *felafel* mix
1¼ cups vegetable oil (for frying)
  1 tomato, chopped
½ cucumber, chopped
½ green pepper, seeded and chopped
¼ small head lettuce, shredded

4 pieces pita bread
4 tablespoons *tahina*, thinned
    according to directions on can

1. Make *felafel* mix according to package directions. Roll into small balls about the size of walnuts.
2. In a deep skillet, heat oil over medium-high heat until hot enough to fry a 1-inch cube of bread in 1 minute. Carefully place balls of *felafel* into oil, a few at a time, and fry 3 to 5 minutes until golden brown on all sides. Remove from oil with slotted spoon and drain on paper towels.
3. In a medium bowl, combine tomato, cucumber, green pepper, and lettuce.
4. Cut each piece of pita bread in half. Into the pocket of each pita, put 3 *felafel* balls and 2 to 3 tablespoons salad mixture. Dribble 1 tablespoon *tahina* over each. Serve immediately.

Serves 4

Felafel in pita and warm Israeli doughnuts coated with powdered sugar are two popular snack foods in Israel.

Israeli Doughnuts/ Soofganiyot

Doughnuts are a favorite seasonal snack, eaten mostly in winter at Hanukah (also called Chanukah). These doughnuts, cooked in oil, commemorate the oil that burned in the ruined Temple in Jerusalem for 8 days, although the supply appeared to be enough only for a single day.
The secret of a really delicious doughnut is the freshness, so fry these just before serving. The dough can be made well ahead of time and refrigerated until ready to use.

2½ **cups all-purpose flour**
  1 **teaspoon baking powder**
  2 **eggs**
1½ **cups (12 ounces) sour cream**
  2 **tablespoons sugar**
  ¼ **teaspoon salt**
  1 **teaspoon vanilla extract**
1¼ **cups vegetable oil (for frying)**
  1 **cup powdered sugar (for coating doughnuts)**

1. In a mixing bowl, combine all ingredients except oil and powdered sugar. The batter will be very soft.
2. In a deep skillet, heat oil until hot enough to fry a 1-inch cube of bread in 1 minute. Carefully place dough, a tablespoon at a time, into oil. Fry doughnuts, a few at a time, 3 to 5 minutes or until golden brown on all sides. Remove from oil with slotted spoon and drain on paper towels.
3. When all doughnuts are fried, pour powdered sugar into a plastic or brown paper bag. Add a few doughnuts at a time, close bag, and shake gently until well coated. Repeat until all doughnuts are coated with sugar. Serve warm.

Makes about 25 doughnuts

Kibbutz carrot salad, flavored with mint and honey, is a delicious addition to a meal of ground meat with sesame sauce and rice.

LUNCH/
Arukhat Tzohorayim

Although lunch can sometimes be a snack meal in the country, it is often quite a large meal in cities and towns. Schoolchildren sometimes eat lunch as late as 2:45 P.M. when the schoolday ends, and some office and shop workers have a break of several hours during the day so that they can go home to eat.

Kibbutz Carrot Salad/
Salat Gezer

Most salads in Israel are prepared right at the table, but this one is prepared ahead of time and served as an appetizer.

2 cups grated carrot
juice of 3 large oranges
(about ½ to ⅔ cup)
juice of 2 lemons (about 6
tablespoons)
½ cup water
4 tablespoons honey
2 sprigs fresh mint for garnish

1. Place grated carrots in a large bowl. Strain orange and lemon juice with a sieve to remove seeds and pour over carrots. Add water and stir in honey.
2. Cover bowl with plastic wrap and refrigerate for at least 2 hours to let flavors blend. Garnish with mint sprigs before serving.

Serves 4

Ground Meat with Sesame Sauce/ Siniyeh

This dish, which is of Yemenite-Jewish origin, is similar to the Greek dish called moussaka, *but uses* tahina *(sesame seed paste) instead of cheese to make it kosher.*

2 pounds ground lamb or beef
2 tablespoons chopped fresh parsley
2 onions, peeled and finely chopped
2 cloves garlic, peeled and crushed
½ teaspoon cinnamon
½ teaspoon salt
¼ teaspoon pepper
2 tablespoons olive oil
2 tablespoons pine nuts
1 cup *tahina*, thinned according to directions on can

1. Preheat oven to 400°.
2. In a large bowl, combine ground meat, parsley, onion, garlic, cinnamon, salt, and pepper. Knead to a paste with hands.

3. Brush a 9- by 9-inch baking dish with 1 tablespoon olive oil. Spread meat mixture evenly in dish.
4. In a small skillet, sauté pine nuts in 1 tablespoon olive oil over medium-high heat, stirring constantly, about 2 to 3 minutes or until lightly browned. Remove skillet from heat as soon as nuts are cooked. Sprinkle nuts and their cooking oil over meat mixture.
5. Bake meat for 30 minutes or until brown on top.
6. Pour *tahina* evenly over meat and bake another 15 minutes or until browned and bubbling. Serve with rice and salad.

Serves 4

Baked Fish/
Dag Bitanoor

Carp is a very popular fish in Israel. They are bred in carp ponds for European Jews, who like freshwater fish. This recipe is also often used for cooking St. Peter's fish, which is found only in the Sea of Galilee (a freshwater lake). For this recipe, you can use carp, trout, or any other freshwater fish.

**4 small white fish fillets,
   about 2 pounds**
½ teaspoon salt
**¼ teaspoon pepper
   juice of ½ lemon (about 1½
      tablespoons)**
2 onions, peeled and sliced
**1 cup (8 ounces) plain yogurt,
   beaten until smooth**

1. Preheat oven to 350°.
2. Grease a 9- by 13-inch baking dish.

3. Wash fish under cold running water and pat dry with paper towels.
4. Place fish in baking dish. Sprinkle with salt, pepper, and lemon juice. Top with onion slices and pour yogurt over fish.
5. Bake fish for 45 minutes or until it flakes easily (do not overcook), basting every 15 minutes with pan juices. Serve with salad and baked potatoes.

Serves 4

Baked fish and fruit soup are made with the fresh, healthy ingredients that are typical of Israeli cooking.

Fruit Soup/
Marak Peirot

This soup probably came from western Russia or the Baltic Republics. It can be served as a first course but is more often served as a dessert. Any combination of soft fruits such as peaches, apricots, pears, plums, or berries can be used. (If using berries, however, omit the raisins.) In Israel, plums are usually used and give the soup a dark, ruby-red color. This soup is delicious topped with sour cream.

**2 pounds fresh fruit, pitted
    or 1 pound dried fruit,
      pitted and soaked overnight
  juice and grated peel of 1
    lemon (about 3 tablespoons juice;
     1½ teaspoons peel)
½ cup sugar
½ cup raisins, soaked
    overnight in just enough
    water to cover
6 cups water
1 tablespoon cornstarch**

1. Cut all fruit except lemon and raisins into 1-inch pieces. Place in large kettle and sprinkle with lemon juice, grated lemon peel, and sugar.
2. Drain raisins, saving soaking water. Add raisins to kettle. In a small bowl, mix raisin soaking water with cornstarch.
3. Pour 6 cups water over fruit. Heat slowly, stirring in cornstarch mixture. Continue to stir until mixture boils.
4. Reduce heat and simmer 5 minutes, stirring constantly. The liquid should thicken slightly.
5. Remove pan from heat and cool soup to room temperature. Pour soup into a glass bowl, cover with plastic wrap, and refrigerate until thoroughly chilled. Serve very cold.

Serves 4 to 6

VEGETARIAN MEAL/ Arukhat Tsimhonit

There are probably proportionally more vegetarians in Israel than anywhere else in the western world. This is due to the poor quality and high price of Israeli meat and also because Israelis are very health conscious and concerned about cruelty to animals. In every institution where people eat in a communal situation, including the *kibbutz* and the army, both vegetarian and meat menus are available.

Cheese Blintzes/ Levavot Gvina

These pancakes, an Israeli version of a Russian dish, are particularly connected with the Jewish Feast of Weeks (Shavuot), when dairy dishes are eaten.

Filling:

1 8-ounce package cream
   cheese, softened

1 cup (8 ounces) cottage cheese
1 egg
½ teaspoon salt
½ cup raisins

Batter:

2 eggs
½ teaspoon salt
1 cup water
1 cup all-purpose flour
6 tablespoons butter or
   margarine

1. In a medium mixing bowl, make filling by combining cream cheese, cottage cheese, egg, and salt. Beat until mixture is fairly smooth. Stir in raisins.
2. In another bowl, beat eggs well. Add salt and water and stir until blended.
3. Place flour in a large mixing bowl. Gradually add egg mixture, beating well with a spoon to prevent lumps from forming.
4. In a frying pan or crepe pan, melt 1 tablespoon butter over medium-high heat. Stir melted butter into batter.

5. Pour ¼ cup batter into pan, quickly swirling pan so a thin, even layer covers the bottom. Cook on one side only until batter is dry and surface begins to bubble.

6. Remove pancake from pan with a spatula and drain on paper towels. Repeat with remaining batter, adding butter or margarine to lightly grease pan when necessary.

7. When all pancakes have been cooked, place 2 to 3 tablespoons filling on center of each. Roll up pancake and fold the sides underneath.

8. Melt any remaining butter or margarine in the pan and quickly sauté pancakes over medium-high heat until brown and crispy. Serve immediately with sour cream.

Makes about 24 blintzes

Cheese blintzes are thin, crispy pancakes wrapped around a rich filling and topped with sour cream.

Russian Salad/
Salat Russi

Israeli cookery changes with each influx of immigration, and the recent immigration from Russia has brought this classic Russian appetizer to Israel. Any leftover vegetables can be added to the basic mixture. If you prefer a less rich dressing, use plain yogurt instead of sour cream. Russian salad is a good picnic food and is delicious with hard-cooked eggs.

1 **cup cooked peas, fresh, frozen, or canned**
1 **cup cooked diced carrots, fresh, frozen, or canned**
4 **new potatoes, boiled in skins and chopped**
1 **small cucumber, peeled and chopped**
1 **kosher dill pickle, finely chopped**
½ **apple, peeled, cored, and finely chopped**
½ **cup canned sliced mushrooms, drained**
4 **lettuce leaves**

Dressing:

1 **tablespoon mayonnaise**
3 **tablespoons sour cream**
1 **teaspoon lemon juice**
1 **teaspoon Dijon-style mustard**
1 **teaspoon dill weed**
¼ **teaspoon salt**
⅛ **teaspoon paprika**

1. In a large bowl, mix peas, carrots, potatoes, cucumber, pickle, apple, and mushrooms.
2. In a small bowl, combine mayonnaise, sour cream, lemon juice, mustard, dill weed, and salt. Beat until smooth.
3. Just before serving, stir dressing into vegetable mixture, tossing lightly until vegetables are evenly coated.
4. Sprinkle salad with paprika and serve on lettuce leaves.

Serves 4

FRIDAY NIGHT DINNER/
Arukhat Erev Shabbat

Because Jews are forbidden to work on the Sabbath, which begins at sundown on Friday, the food for Friday evening is prepared during daylight hours and kept warm until the Sabbath begins.

Bean Soup/
Marak Shu'it

This simple soup is a wintertime favorite. Israelis use Egyptian field beans because they are the most easily available. The soup can be made with any kind of bean, however, such as navy or kidney beans.

1 onion, peeled and chopped
3 tablespoons vegetable oil
1 15-ounce can beans, undrained
1 6-ounce can tomato puree
2 10¾-ounce cans (about 3 cups) beef broth
3 cloves garlic, chopped
½ teaspoon salt
¼ teaspoon pepper
2 tablespoons chopped fresh parsley
3 cups water

1. In a medium skillet, heat oil over medium-high heat. Add onion and sauté until transparent but not brown. Place onion in a large kettle.
2. Add beans, tomato puree, beef broth, garlic, salt, pepper, and parsley to kettle. Stir in 3 cups water.
3. Bring soup to a boil over high heat, stirring occasionally. Reduce heat, cover kettle, and simmer for 20 minutes.
4. Serve hot with pita bread.

Serves 4 to 6

Turkey schnitzel, with its crunchy matzo coating, and hearty bean soup are two dishes that can be served as part of a Sabbath meal.

Turkey Schnitzel/ Schnitzel Hodoo

This is a variation of the famous Wiener (Vienna) schnitzel *served in Austria and Germany. In Europe, this dish is made with slices of veal. In Israel, veal is scarce and expensive, so instead Israelis use turkey breast, which has a similar flavor. You can find slices of uncooked turkey in the meat section of your supermarket, or you can buy a whole uncooked turkey breast and have it sliced. The addition of matzo meal to the batter is a typically Jewish touch and adds a nice crunchiness.*

8 slices uncooked turkey breast
½ teaspoon salt
¼ teaspoon pepper
1 teaspoon onion powder
1 teaspoon ground cumin
2 eggs
2 tablespoons water
½ cup all-purpose flour
½ cup matzo meal
½ cup vegetable oil (for frying)

lemon slices and parsley for garnish

1. Place each slice of meat between two pieces of waxed paper and beat with a hammer to flatten. Remove paper and sprinkle both sides of meat with salt, pepper, onion powder, and cumin.
2. In a flat dish, beat together eggs and 2 tablespoons water. Pour flour into another flat dish and matzo meal into a third flat dish.
3. In a large skillet, heat oil over medium-high heat until hot enough to brown a 1-inch cube of bread in 1 minute. Dip a slice of meat into egg mixture, coating it thoroughly. Then dip it lightly in the flour and finally in the matzo meal. The slices should be completely covered with batter on both sides.
4. Fry meat about 7 minutes per side or until brown and crisp. Drain on paper towels. Garnish with slices of lemon and sprigs of parsley. Serve hot with mashed or french fried potatoes.

Serves 4

Poppy Seed Cake/
Ugat Pereg

In Israel, one can always expect company, invited or not, after the Friday evening meal. This is a good cake to have on hand to serve visitors. A 12-ounce can of prune filling can be substituted for the poppy seed. (If you use one of the new quick-acting yeasts, follow package directions instead of the instructions given here.)

Batter:

½ **cup milk**
1 **envelope active dry yeast**
1 **tablespoon sugar**
2 **cups all-purpose flour, plus**
    extra for rolling dough
½ **cup butter or margarine, softened**
1 **12-ounce can poppy seed filling**

1. In a small saucepan, scald milk over low heat. Remove from heat and let cool slightly.
2. Warm a small cup or bowl by rinsing in hot water and drying thoroughly. In warmed bowl, combine yeast with 1 teaspoon sugar and 1 tablespoon flour. Add warm milk and stir until dissolved. Cover with a cloth and leave in a warm place for about 20 minutes or until mixture foams.
3. In a large bowl, beat together butter and remaining sugar until smooth. Gradually add remaining flour, beating constantly. Stir in yeast mixture.
4. Place dough on floured wooden board or countertop. Knead for about 15 minutes, adding enough flour to produce an elastic dough that is no longer sticky.
5. Wash out bowl with hot water, dry thoroughly, and grease. Return dough to bowl, cover with plastic wrap, and leave in a warm place to rise for 1 hour. (This is a rather dry dough and will not rise much.)
6. Preheat oven to 400°.
7. Sprinkle wooden board or countertop with more flour. With a floured rolling pin, roll out dough into an 8- by 10-inch rectangle. Spread poppy seed filling

evenly over dough, leaving a margin of about ½ inch around edges. Starting at one of the long sides, roll up dough jelly-roll fashion.

8. Grease cookie sheet. Slide cake carefully onto the cookie sheet, turning it so the seam is underneath to keep filling from escaping during baking. Cover cake with a damp kitchen towel and leave in a warm place for 1 hour.

9. Uncover cake and bake for 10 minutes. Then reduce heat to 375° and bake for 30 minutes or until golden brown.

10. Remove cake from oven and let cool completely before transferring to a wire rack.

Frosting:

2 cups powdered sugar
1 egg white, lightly beaten
½ teaspoon lemon juice
¼ to ½ cup water

1. Sift powdered sugar into a medium mixing bowl. Make a well in center of sugar and pour egg white and lemon juice into it. Gradually mix powdered sugar into liquid with a spoon, adding water little by little until frosting is smooth. (Frosting should be thick enough to coat the back of a spoon.)

2. When completely smooth, pour frosting over cake, letting it dribble down the sides.

Makes about 30 slices

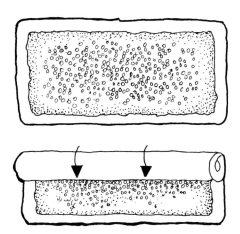

SATURDAY MIDDAY MEAL/ Arukhat Tzohorayim Bishabbat

The Sabbath meal is always a formal occasion. The table is laid with a white cloth and the best dishes and silverware are used. Unless the Sabbath falls during the week of Shavuot— the Feast of Weeks—when dairy products are traditionally eaten, or unless the family is vegetarian, some kind of meat dish is served in even the poorest households. Every Jewish community has its own Sabbath dishes, which are prepared on Friday afternoon and then kept warm until the next day.

Sabbath Stew/ Dfina

Israel's many Jews eat slow-cooked stews on the Sabbath. Put in the oven on Friday before nightfall, the stew cooks overnight and is eaten for lunch the next day after the morning synagogue service. All of these stews contain meat and white beans of some type and are very nutritious. This version is from Egypt and is characterized by the hard-cooked eggs, which will have delicious, creamy yolks from cooking so slowly.

1¼ cups (½ pound) chickpeas
1¼ cups (½ pound) navy beans
4 tablespoons vegetable oil
2 large onions, peeled and
    finely chopped
6 small new potatoes, peeled
2 pounds beef (flank steak,
    short ribs or brisket),
    cut into 2-inch cubes
8 uncooked eggs in their shells
4 cloves garlic, finely chopped
1 teaspoon ground coriander
1 teaspoon ground cumin
1 teaspoon allspice
1 teaspoon salt
½ teaspoon pepper

1. Place chickpeas and navy beans in separate bowls. Add enough water to

each bowl to just cover and soak overnight.

2. Preheat oven to 375°.

3. In a medium skillet, heat oil over medium-high heat and sauté onions until golden brown.

4. Place potatoes, onions, meat, and eggs in their shells into a large ovenproof pot or casserole with a tight-fitting lid. (Be careful not to break eggs.) Drain chickpeas and beans, discarding soaking liquid, and add them to the pot. Add garlic, coriander, cumin, and allspice and mix well.

5. Add enough water to pot to barely cover contents. If lid of pot does not fit tightly, put a layer of foil between pot and lid.

6. Bake stew for 1 hour. Stir in salt and pepper. Reduce heat to lowest setting and cook for 5 to 8 hours.

7. Remove eggs from shells and cut into quarters. Serve stew hot, garnished with egg.

Serves 8

Slow-cooked Sabbath stew will satisfy even the largest of appetites.

PASSOVER MEAL/ Seder

The Seder is the traditional feast of Passover. It consists of a ritual meal in which certain foods must be served. A special dish on the table contains 3 matzos, a roast leg of lamb, roasted egg, salt water, bitter herbs, a sweet paste called *charoset*, and a green herb, usually parsley or lettuce. Each of these foods is symbolic of Passover. The salt water represents the tears shed by the Children of Israel in their slavery and the *charoset* is symbolic of the mortar used by the Jewish slaves in Egypt to bind the bricks. Four ritual glasses of wine are drunk during the meal, and an extra cup (and sometimes an extra place setting) is reserved for the Prophet Elijah, who Jews believe will bring the promised Messiah.

North African Chicken Soup/ Marak Off Mizarahi

Chicken soup has a special place in Jewish life all over the world. This soup is prepared as in North Africa—tangy, lemony, and peppery. If the chicken meat is eaten separately, it is eaten with rice, as North African Sephardic Jews are allowed to eat rice on Passover. (The Jews of German origin, called Ashkenazim, are forbidden rice on Passover.)

1 **large chicken (at least 3 pounds)**
3 **lemons**
2 **small turnips, peeled**
3 **onions, peeled (1 stuck
    with 2 whole cloves)**
2 **carrots, peeled and sliced
    lengthwise**
1 **bunch parsley, with root if
    possible, or 1 small
    parsnip, peeled, or both**
2 **teaspoons salt**
½ **teaspoon pepper**

1 teaspoon cinnamon
1 teaspoon chili powder
**¼ teaspoon powdered saffron
     or turmeric**
2 eggs, beaten

1. Wash chicken. Squeeze juice from one of the lemons into a small bowl and set aside. Rub chicken all over with the inside of a squeezed lemon half. Place chicken in a large, deep kettle and add enough water to barely cover it.
2. Bring water in kettle to a boil over high heat. With a spoon, skim off the foam that forms on the surface of the water.
3. When you have removed as much foam as possible and the water is boiling, reduce heat and add vegetables, parsley, salt, and pepper. Cover kettle and let chicken simmer 1 hour.
4. Add lemon juice and remaining spices to soup. Cover kettle and simmer for another hour.
5. With tongs, carefully remove chicken from pot. Place on a plate and let cool. When cool, remove meat from bones and set aside.
6. Carefully pour broth through a sieve with another large pan underneath to catch liquid. Save the vegetables.
7. Cool broth to room temperature, then refrigerate for 30 minutes to bring fat to the surface. Skim the surface with a paper towel to absorb fat.
8. Before serving, beat eggs into 1 cup of the soup and return to kettle. Add the cooked vegetables and, if desired, bite-size pieces of the cooked chicken. (The chicken can also be served separately.) Reheat soup, stirring occasionally. Do not let it boil.
9. Serve soup hot with remaining lemons cut into wedges for squeezing into soup.

Serves 6 to 8

Chicken stuffed with oranges can be served with matzo at Passover or with challah, a traditional bread, for a Sabbath meal.

Chicken Stuffed with Oranges/ Off Memooleh Betapoozim

This is an adaptation of a prize-winning recipe from a contest organized by the Israeli Touring Club in Jerusalem many years ago. It combines the most popular and economical ingredients in an Israeli meal: citrus fruit and chicken.

1 2½- to 3-pound chicken
1 lemon
2 teaspoons salt
1 teaspoon garlic powder
2 teaspoons paprika
1 teaspoon chili powder
1 teaspoon ground coriander
2 oranges
1 cup water
2 onions, peeled

1. Preheat oven to 425°.
2. Rinse chicken inside and out under cold running water. Pat dry with paper towels.
3. Place chicken in a roasting pan. Cut lemon in half and rub one half over surface of chicken.
4. In a small bowl, mix spices together and sprinkle over chicken.
5. Squeeze juice from lemon half and from 1 of the oranges into roasting pan and add water. Place remaining orange, whole and unpeeled, in chicken cavity. Cut onions in half and add to pan.
6. Cook chicken for 15 minutes, then baste with the pan juices and lower heat to 350°. Cook for 1 hour, basting after 30 minutes.
7. Remove orange from cavity of chicken. Cut orange and onions into small pieces and serve with chicken. This dish is delicious with rice or pasta.

Serves 4 to 6

Passover matzo layer cake and melon dessert are two simple, yet festive, ways to end a meal.

Passover Matzo Layer Cake/ Ugat Matzot

During Passover, this cake is made with potato starch instead of cornstarch, which is forbidden at this time. Halva is a sticky-sweet candy—a hard block of nuts ground with sugar and honey. The best halva is made from almonds, but you can also buy sesame and peanut halva. Halva can be purchased at any Greek, Middle Eastern, or Jewish market.

6 tablespoons sugar
4 squares unsweetened chocolate
1 cup water
1 stick (¼ pound) butter or
  margarine, cut into pieces
6 ounces *halva*, cut into small pieces
2 tablespoons potato starch or
  cornstarch
6 large matzos
  colored candy sprinkles for
  decoration

1. In a medium saucepan, combine sugar, chocolate, and water. Cook over medium-high heat, stirring constantly, until chocolate is completely melted and mixture comes to a boil.
2. Add butter and *halva*. Continue stirring until mixture boils again, then remove pan from the heat.
3. In a small bowl, mix potato starch with 2 tablespoons water and stir into chocolate mixture. Cook over medium heat, stirring until mixture thickens. Remove pan from heat.
4. Put 1 matzo on a platter large enough to let it lie flat. Spread an even layer of chocolate mixture over matzo. Place another matzo on top and cover with more of the chocolate mixture. Repeat with remaining matzos, finishing with a layer of chocolate. Scatter sprinkles over cake for decoration.
5. Refrigerate cake overnight so chocolate mixture will harden and flavors will mingle. To serve, cut cake with a sharp knife into 1- by 2-inch rectangles.

Serves 10

Melon Dessert/
Liftan Melon

Israeli melons are small cantaloupe-style melons called Ogen melons. They are named for the kibbutz *where they were first grown.*

2 small cantaloupes
½ pound green grapes
½ pound red grapes
4 peaches
1 teaspoon cinnamon
1 cup white grape juice

1. Cut melons in half. Scrape out and discard seeds. Scrape out most of the melon flesh, being careful not to pierce the skin.
2. With a melon baller, cut melon flesh into small balls, or cut it into small pieces with a sharp knife.
3. Wash grapes and remove from stems. (If grapes have seeds, cut fruit in half and discard seeds.) Save four tiny clusters of red grapes for decoration.
4. Half fill a medium saucepan with water and bring to a boil over high heat. Carefully place peaches into boiling water. After 5 minutes, remove them with a slotted spoon. When peaches are cool enough to handle, peel and cut into small pieces.
5. In a large bowl, combine cinnamon, grape juice, melon, grapes, and peaches and stir. Spoon mixture back into melon shells. Top with reserved grape clusters. Refrigerate and serve cold.

Serves 4

THE CAREFUL COOK

Whenever you cook, there are certain safety rules you must always keep in mind. Even experienced cooks follow these rules when they are in the kitchen.

1. Always wash your hands before handling food.
2. Thoroughly wash all raw vegetables and fruits to remove dirt, chemicals, and insecticides.
3. Use a cutting board when cutting up vegetables and fruits. Don't cut them up in your hand! And be sure to cut in a direction *away* from you and your fingers.
4. Long hair or loose clothing can easily catch fire if brought near the burners of a stove. If you have long hair, tie it back before you start cooking.
5. Turn all pot handles toward the back of the stove so that you will not catch your sleeve or jewelry on them. This is especially important when younger brothers and sisters are around. They could easily knock off a pot and get burned.
6. Always use a pot holder to steady hot pots or to take pans out of the oven. Don't use a wet cloth on a hot pan because the steam it produces could burn you.
7. Lift the lid of a steaming pot with the opening away from you so that you will not get burned.
8. If you get burned, hold the burn under cold running water. Do not put grease or butter on it. Cold water helps to take the heat out, but grease or butter will only keep it in.
9. If grease or cooking oil catches fire, throw baking soda or salt at the bottom of the flame to put it out. (Water will *not* put out a grease fire.) Call for help and try to turn all the stove burners to "off."

RECIPE NAMES IN THE HEBREW ALPHABET

Israeli Salad / Salat Yisraeli / סלט ישראלי

Egg and Tomato Scramble / Shakshooka / שקשוקה

Felafel in Pita / Felafel Bipita / פלאפל בפיטה

Israeli Doughnuts / Soofganiyot / סופגניות

Kibbutz Carrot Salad / Salat Gezer / סלט גזר

Ground Meat with Sesame Sauce / Siniyeh / סינייה

Baked Fish / Dag Bitanoor / דג בתנור

Fruit Soup / Marak Peirot / מרק פירות

Cheese Blintzes / Levavot Gvina / לבבות גבינה

Russian Salad / Salat Russi / סלט רוסי

Bean Soup / Marak Shu'it / מרק שעועית

Turkey Schnitzel / Schnitzel Hodoo / שניצל הודו

Poppy Seed Cake / Ugat Pereg / עוגת פרג

Sabbath Stew / Dfina / דפינה

North African Chicken Soup / Marak Off Mizarahi / מרק עוף מזרחי

Chicken Stuffed with Oranges / Off Memooleh Betapoozim / עוף ממולה בתפוזים

Passover Matzo Layer Cake / Ugat Matzot / עוגת מצות

Melon Dessert / Liftan Melon / לפתן מילון

Breakfast / Arukhat Boker / ארוחת בוקר

Snacks / Mata'amim / מתעמים

Lunch / Arukhat Tzohorayim / ארוחת צהרים

Vegetarian Meal / Arukhat Tsimhonit / ארוחת צמחונית

Friday Night Dinner / Arukhat Erev Shabbat / ארוחת צהרים שבת

Saturday Midday Meal / Arukhat Tzohorayim Bishabbat / ארוחת צהרים בשבת

Passover Meal / Seder / ארוחת ליל הסדר

METRIC CONVERSION CHART

WHEN YOU KNOW		MULTIPLY BY	TO FIND	
MASS (weight)				
ounces	(oz)	28.0	grams	(g)
pounds	(lb)	0.45	kilograms	(kg)
VOLUME				
teaspoons	(tsp)	5.0	milliliters	(ml)
tablespoons	(Tbsp)	15.0	milliliters	
fluid ounces	(oz)	30.0	milliliters	
cup	(c)	0.24	liters	(l)
pint	(pt)	0.47	liters	
quart	(qt)	0.95	liters	
gallon	(gal)	3.8	liters	
TEMPERATURE				
Fahrenheit	(°F)	5/9 (after	Celsius	(°C)
temperature		subtracting 32)	temperature	

COMMON MEASURES AND THEIR EQUIVALENTS

3 teaspoons = 1 tablespoon

8 tablespoons = ½ cup

2 cups = 1 pint

2 pints = 1 quart

4 quarts = 1 gallon

16 ounces = 1 pound

INDEX

(recipes indicated by **bold face** *type)*

ABOUT THE AUTHOR

Josephine Bacon is an Israeli who now lives in Anaheim, California. She has written about Israeli cooking for many publications, including the *Los Angeles Herald Examiner.* In addition to writing about food, Bacon is a professional Hebrew translator and courtroom interpreter and also teaches cooking at a community college in Southern California.

Poppy seed cake can be made with either prune or poppy seed filling. (Recipe on page 36.)